GWANGUNG

Presents

Dynamic wall bag Training guide

The Complete Wall Bag Training Guide

By GWANGUNG

First published 2010

ISBN 978-1-4452-9043-0

Please note that the author and publisher of this book are NOT RESPONSIBLE in any manner what so ever for any injury that may result from practicing any techniques and / or following the instructions within. Since the physical activities described herein may be to strenuous or hard in nature for some readers to engage in safely. It is essential that a physician be consulted before training starts.

Acknowledgements

The Chinese martial arts have many families and this book would not have been possible with out the help and co-operation of the many Chinese martial arts instructors, coaches and experts that we interviewed. We would like to thank all of them for sharing their advice, knowledge and expertise with us. We would also like to thank all of the students and instructors that train every week in their endless pursuit for perfection while keeping Chinese martial arts alive.

Chinese Proverb

"Teachers open the door, but you must enter by yourself"

Table of contents

How this book came about

Gwangung have been a major supplier to the Chinese martial arts for over 10 years. In our journey to supply the best for the best, we have sourced some of the best traditional weapons manufacturers in northern and southern china. We have supplied these traditional weapons and training equipment to martial arts clubs, instructors, students, shops and film sets all over the UK and Europe. We have seen the traditional Chinese martial arts evolve and grow through out the years.

This book has been produced by Gwangung because of demand. We had been approached by a lot of our customers, people we spoke to and clubs that buy from us. They were all looking for a way to develop that 'snap' or extra 'chi' (power) in their punches or strikes, while toughening their hands to help deliver this kind of strike. They were buying the canvas wall bags and filling them with all kinds of things in an effort to help harden and develop that missing 'chi' for their kung fu. So we started to provide ready filled, heavy duty canvas wall bags with a range of different fillings, but we felt just selling these wall bags to martial arts schools, instructors and students was not enough, there was no books, DVD's or reference guides available for conditioning and wall bag training. So we want to help you on your journey to attain the best from your training that you possibly can. We want you to train safe; we want to help you condition your hands and develop that 'chi' power that is missing from your training.

After a lot of research and a large amount of interviews with martial arts expert's, instructors and coaches, we have brought you a comprehensive guide which is not style orientated. The research was taken from a study of a wide range of different Chinese martial arts styles. It is 'traditional' orientated. It is full of punching and striking techniques which have been used from ancient times. This book covers vital information for the best available modern day equipment, the best natural wall bag fillings, conditioning drills, techniques and routines, striking techniques, essential oils and balms and much more. This book will outline some of the best techniques needed to help you attain 'chi' power.

Introduction

One of the main elements of any martial art is the ability to hit, strike or punch effectively, training against a punch bag, focus mitts or strike shield is all well and good but when you really need to defend your self, when you really need to hit, strike or punch for real, in a real situation. Then as we know or should know the hitting, striking and punching takes on a completely different meaning than in any training hall or gym. It can sometimes be the difference between life or death, all that training, all them hours standing in a low stance practicing punches, running through forms or katas, working on training drills, attending gradings, all for that moment.

During our research we lost count of the number of interviews that we conducted where the martial artists who found themselves, there, in that very situation, throws that vital punch, the one and only chance, the technique is perfect, it should be, as it had been drilled hundreds if not thousands of times in class, that ultimate strike……result?...NO effect what so ever, the offender ran straight through it as if it wasn't there....Why I hear you ask?......Conditioning….while we go through training drills, technique and applications, that vital punch, that very strike has to have the impact of a hammer, the assailant needs to feel that he has been hit by an express train. He is just as high on adrenalin as you, probably more so, he might even be a more experienced seasoned street fighter whose knuckles have been broken many times through his many fights. So what do you hit him with? The truth of the matter is that if you have not done any conditioning, if you have not drilled your punches, strikes or techniques into a sand or wall bag, then you might as well hit him with a lettuce. Your knuckles, fingers and hands will crinkle up like a bag of biscuits. Sorry to be blunt, but have you ever tried to hit a nail into a piece of wood with a rubber hammer. The nail goes further into the rubber hammer head than the wood. 'Same principle'.

The people we interviewed took time to show us their lumps and bumps from previously broken knuckles and fingers. In many cases it made them look upon their training from a completely different angle. They started to re-evaluate how they practiced and drilled their martial arts techniques.

They also looked at what worked for them and what did not. They understood what was needed, should they ever find them selves in the same situation again. Some of the instructor stopped training for a while, shocked by what had happened, they had been black belt instructors for years under a egotistical illusion inflated by all the students that had looked up to them thinking that they were the ultimate street warrior, that what ever they practiced in class worked on the streets. What it really did is gave them a reality check.

Sand and gravel filled wall bags suddenly started to play a bigger part in their martial arts training.

Most martial artists have heard of iron palm training. The idea that we can toughen our hands to the point of delivering bone crushing blows appeals to our sense of being the ultimately deadly warrior. Unfortunately the majority of martial artists will never have the opportunity to train under an iron palm master or even want to dedicate their life to endless hours of striking trees, bricks or tiles day after day.

With this wall bag training and conditioning guide you will learn the traditional strikes and punching styles from a selection of Chinese martial arts. Their training drills, techniques and their basic conditioning principles to safely condition and toughen your hands. To help prevent injuries during sparring, wall bag training or self defense situations.

Anyone who has hurt their hands knows that injured fingers or injured hands slows down training and can be a major setback if the injury is serious enough. It is not uncommon to injure hands, fingers or knuckles at some point during your training or sparring. Permanent hand injuries not only prevent you from being able to punch effectively but can also affect other aspects or martial arts techniques such as grappling, hand trapping. Having tougher hands may prevent injuries, so not to hinder your training progress, beside you need your hands in good shape for your job and when you get older you want to maintain the dexterity and flexibility of your fingers. Even shaolin monks didn't turn their hands to unbending clubs from their training. They toughened them to the point where they could rip the bark off trees yet maintained the flexibility so that they could practice other cultural arts such as calligraphy.

Brief history

Throughout the history of Chinese martial arts, the practice of hardening the body, hands and feet has been an integral part of basic training. Kung Fu practitioners needed some way to improve their power, their ability to withstand blows, and their ability to inflict great damage on their opponents, all without causing any damage to themselves. Necessity is the mother of invention, and this is why "Iron" training evolved.

China has been the source of many legends, mysteries, and ancient secrets, none more so than the ability to destroy solid objects with the human hands such as granite stones, bricks or tiles. Some of the most amazing demonstrations witnessed, has to be the ability to destroy a single brick or tile within a pile with out breaking any other in the same pile. This ability to direct the power to one point within a pile of bricks or tiles has taken years to generate and direct,

Until the early part of this century, practitioners of Iron Palm were not as eager to show off their skill as today's Iron Palm practitioners are. Their life depended on their skill, so they did not want to reveal their "secret weapon." The main reason why public Iron Palm demonstrations are common today can be traced back to the Northern Shaolin Grand Teacher Ku Yu Cheong, one of the most famous Kung Fu masters of the first half of the Twentieth Century. Prior to World War II, martial arts were neither as important nor as popular as they once were and an effort was being made by the Chinese government to revive their popularity. The government sought to rid themselves of the "sick man of Asia" stigma by recruiting well know martial arts teachers and deploying them throughout the country to promote and teach their arts for health and fitness. After moving to Guangzhou to teach, Ku Yu Cheong chose to advance the Northern Shaolin system by taking part in demonstrations showcasing the differences between the Chinese martial styles. To prove himself and gain students, he gave many performances, most of which included demonstrations of his Iron Body and Iron Palm techniques. One of the most famous pictures of Ku Yu Cheung that survives today shows him breaking a stack of 10 bricks without any spacers between the bricks.

Demonstrations of this amazing ability are seldom seen or performed by the martial artists of today.

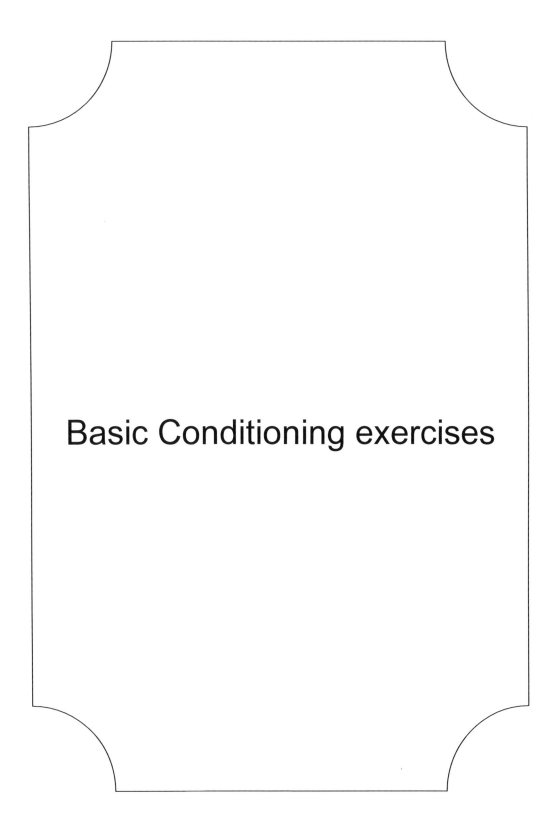

Basic Conditioning exercises

Choi, Hong Hi, Founder of Taekwon-Do

"Pain is the best instructor, but no one wants to go to his class."

Basic conditioning

When we interviewed the martial arts instructors and coaches there was a mixed reaction to the issue of when to begin conditioning training and working out on the wall bag. At some martial arts schools, a student must train for 3 years before he will be introduced to hard conditioning. Other schools believe that this sort of training should be started as soon as the student grasps the basics (stances and such). Each of these schools of thought has its advantages:

Starting conditioning after a few years, makes sure that the student is well drilled and will have mastered the basics behind the techniques and applications from their chosen art, plus the instructor knows by then that the student has show a reasonable amount of dedication which is a good measure to introduce the conditioning and wall bag drills.

 Conditioning and wall bag drills early has its advantages as well. The main idea behind this is that the student will be able to defend himself better once he has spent some time training. Of course, no kung fu school would begin conditioning training from day one, but under this idea it can reasonably be expected to start after the student has learned the basics (such as the various stances, strikes, etc.). Additionally, in some martial arts wall bag training may be integral to the system and waiting to begin that portion of the training would cause a gap in the student's knowledge of his art. Essentially, there needs to be an agreement between the student and the teacher as to when is the correct time to learn. It's just another aspect that must be taken into consideration both when a student is choosing a school and when a sifu is choosing a student.

When conditioning and wall bag training is done correctly there should be no loss of sensitivity in the hands. A common misconception is that the constant training and hitting of the bag damages the nerves in the hand. Some martial artists do train in this manner, but it isn't healthy, In fact, this concept can be used as a gauge by which to evaluate a potential martial arts instructor's credentials. For example, if your teacher tells you that you must sacrifice the sensation in your hands in order to develop as a martial artist, you might want to think about looking elsewhere for instruction.

Basic conditioning for martial artists does not have to be tuff or painful, it takes time, slow gradual progress and regular training is the true key. There is no quick fix, no short cut, but there is no need to go to extremes, such as driving your hands in to hot sands or iron filings, or breaking tiles and bricks.

Conditioning the hands

For many martial artists the canvas wall bags are the ideal traditional training tool. They can be filled with a variety of fillings so you can either lay them on the floor or bench for conditioning exercises or hang them on the wall to drill your striking and punching techniques while visualizing the applications.

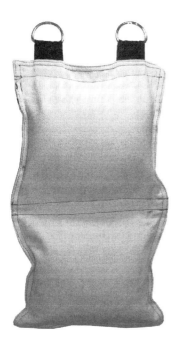 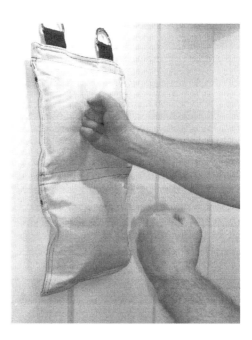

 Most wall or conditioning bags in present day are normally made from heavy duty canvas, you can still get nylon weave canvas, leather or leatherette wall bags but none of these wear as well as the natural heavy duty canvas wall bags and the texture of the natural canvas helps to harden and prepare the skin covering the striking areas.

Also some wall bags have interesting designs on them e.g. Bruce lee images or target areas, which sometimes helps with visualization when training, but a quick note about the effective hanging fixings at the top of the wall bags is that some wall bags have holes across the top or around the sides.

These type of bags are fine when on the ground but through our years of supplying these products we have found that when they are hung up on a wall or suspended from these holes, with all the heavy filling and constant striking, over time the round eyelet's that line the holes tends to come away from the canvas and allows the bag to rip. The best type of hangings that we have found, have the heavy duty straps and 'D' rings.

Wall bags differ in size and the amount of section.

First you have the single section canvas wall bag which is ideal for hanging on the wall or laying down either on the ground or bench for conditioning exercises, which we will cover later on. Then you have the two wall bag and three section wall bag. These offer you the chance to fill each section with different fillings giving you a selection of densities.

Three section   Two section   Single section

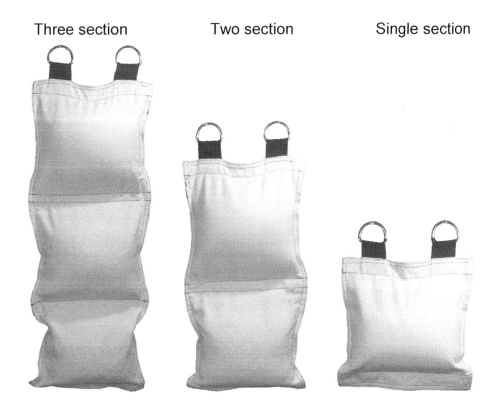

Wall Bag Fillings

Fillings vary depending on certain requirements such as preferences, martial art styles or personal abilities. Some of the more modern day and common fillings we can find either at most diy stores, builders merchants or hard wear shops.

It is always best practiced that before any fillings are placed within the sections of the canvas wall bags, you insert a liner such as a small carrier bag and then fill the carrier bag while it is within the wall bag section. When it is as full as you require, tie the bag, sealing it with a knot and close the zip, this firstly protects the zip and stops any dust coming through the bag when striking and makes it easier to change the filling if required later on.

Sand is a common filling which gives a relatively soft resistance. Filling at least one section of your wall bag with sand is a good start, not just any sand. Some sands have a larger grit level which we will go into more detail later. It is best filled with kiln dried sand. This makes an ideal filling as it offers a good resistance and helps the bag regain its shape after training, also it moves when struck, resembling the kind of resistance and densities that you would get when striking the softer parts of a human body.

The next grade filling that we recommend is 10mm gravel or pea gravel, this allows a more controlled resistance slightly denser than the kiln dried sand but it gives you a slightly sharp edge when struck.

When pea gravel is mixed with kiln dried sand, 50% pea gravel, 50% kiln dried sand then this gives you a medium density between the two, as adding the sand helps the gravel to move.

So with just these two types of fillings, kiln dried sand and gravel you can easily produce the main three different densities that a relative beginner or intermediate martial artist will need.

Gravel over 10mm is not advisable for the average beginner as it does not move very well as the smaller gravel when struck.

Other fillings that you can either use or that we have heard of people using but not always easily available are dried peas, rice, dried beans, saw dust, rags, granite chipping, granite dust, lead shot, ball bearings the list seems endless. We have just shown you two relative easy to find filling which will give you three different resistances and will not leave you short in the pocket.

A single wall bag is great if filled with sand and used as a catch and grab bag when training for grappling and also when filled and hung with either chain or rope and used for finger striking. Which we will cover later in this book

Basic essential conditioning techniques

To get the most from your wall bag training, we want to show you some basic conditioning techniques that will help you develop more powerful and stronger hands with fewer injuries. But first we need to warm up to get the blood flowing and muscles relaxed. You should start by first gently.

1) Twisting or slightly rotating the waist from side to side, the waist carries the power from good foundation footwork through to the shoulders.

2) Rolling shoulders round in a circular motion from front and back and then back to front. Stiff or tense shoulders stem the flow of natural power from the good foundation footwork and flexible waist.

3) Rolling the elbows in a circular motion, stiff elbows are like stiff shoulders, them stem the flow of energy so making any technique delivered, lack power.

4) Stretching the wrists up and then down then rolling and flexing them in a circular motion. See (fig 1, 2, 3)

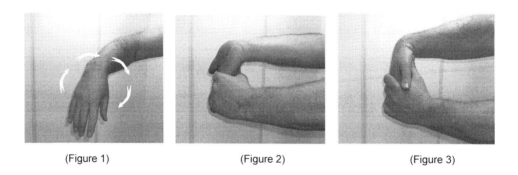

(Figure 1)   (Figure 2)   (Figure 3)

5) Flexing the hands fully open and then tightly closed several times and then massaging in between the bones of the hands See (fig 4, 5)

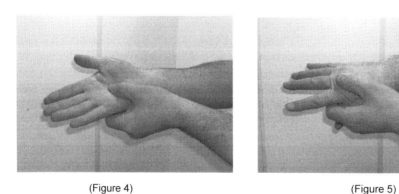

(Figure 4)   (Figure 5)

6) Finally shake the hands and wrists.

Push-ups are a great exercise for building up the shoulders, arms and wrists. But if you find normal push-ups (spanning from the toes to the hands) hard then try shorter push-ups (spanning from the knees to the hands).

Start with 10 reps on the flat of you palm and then if you are feeling confident follow up them with 10 reps on the knuckles of clenched fists and then try 10 reps on the back of the hands but only for the more advanced students. (Over 18's).

We must point out that these basic conditioning techniques and exercises should be practiced in a relax manner. First of all use a stool or any flat surface that can with stand heavy a pounding.

Place a single section wall bag filled with kiln dried sand or rice on the surface in front of you. Make sure that there straps and 'D' rings are folded out of the way and that there is plenty of room around the stool or bench.

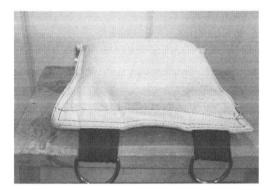

Get into a horse stance (legs shoulder width and bend your knees as if you are ridding a horse, toes pointing forward) facing the bag about two feet away from the bench or bag (depending on the length of your arms). The hand should start approximately 18" inches above the bag and only under the weight of the arm dropping down on the bag should the first strike be delivered.

Three step conditioning exercise

Through out our research and with the feed back that we got from the traditional Chinese martial arts instructors, we have put together a set of short 'three step' light hand conditioning exercise routines which covers preparation and basic conditioning for the punching and striking techniques that will follow as you progress through this book.

After each three step conditioning set shake your hands and then massage from the wrists through the hand and along the fingers and then up the forearms. If at any point during these conditioning routines, you feel any pain or discomfort then stop and seek medical advice before you carry on.

Another important point is to breathe in when raising the arm and always breathe out when dropping the hand down on the surface, releasing any tension.

The first three step conditioning exercise

The first set starts with dropping your hand down with a flat open palm facing down, (figure 6) then lifting back up to the same height and drop, this time with the palm facing up, (figure 7) so contact with the bag using the back of the hand then up same height and drop your hand down with the outer edge of your hand making contact with the knife edge of your hand, thumb facing up. (Figure 8) So you have three relaxed strikes or drops of the arm, open palm, back of the hand, edge of the hand, and then change hands. Do not use force; instead allow the weight of the arm to drop onto the bag with a relaxed hand. Concentrate your attention on the bag. Five reps on each hand is a good start.

(Figure 6)

(Figure 7)

(Figure 8)

The second three step conditioning set

The second set starts with dropping the hand with the palm facing down but slightly raises the fingers (figure 9) so that contact is only made with the heel of the palm, then rise the arm back up and drop the hand with the tiger claw strike (figure 10), raise again and then lift the elbow up and drop the hand using the panther fist (figure 11). When lifting the elbow resist the urge to put power into the panther fist.

We might keep stressing this part but remember when conditioning training, stay relaxed and allow your hand to drop onto the surface, at this point do not tense the arm or shoulder, or exert power while striking. Exerting power or failing to breathe out when dropping your hand onto the surface creates internal stress which is said to be stressful to the heart.

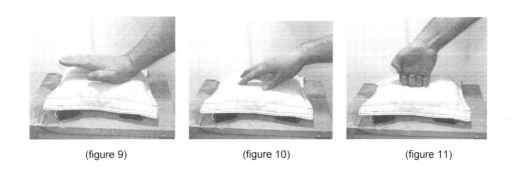

(figure 9)　　　　　　　(figure 10)　　　　　　　(figure 11)

The third and final three step conditioning set

This third and final three step starts with dropping your hand in a hammer fist, (figure 12) then lifting and dropping with a gwi choy fist (back fist) (figure 13) and then lifting and dropping with a normal vertical fist (figure 8).

Through out our research we had a variety of suggestions from different martial arts schools and instructors, regarding conditioning routines, some claiming that their way was the oldest and most traditional.

We have put together this basic conditioning routine using tried and tested conditioning routines.

If you wanted to start setting your own conditioning routine then one of the important points that you need to consider is that certain strikes are used more than others depending on such things as styles, preferences and body types. So if this three step conditioning plan does not fit with your style, preferences or body type then go ahead and develop your own conditioning plan but always make the basic core elements of your conditioning routine a variety of different strikes and punches from your fighting style or body type. Do not fall into the trap of thinking that one style holds all of the answers. This is the reason why we conducted this research to show you the varieties from different styles of martial arts and their advantages.

(Figure 12)   (Figure 13)   (Figure 14)

To make any conditioning routine effective, you need to practice it regularly. You should set your self time slots before you start your main training. Do this for approximately 10 minutes on each conditioning session.

Some of the other interesting conditioning routines that we came across when we conducted our research, was that some schools of eagle claw or tiger style kung fu would fill canvas bags with small stones and toss them to each other and catch them with one hand to condition and develop there grip and finger tips.

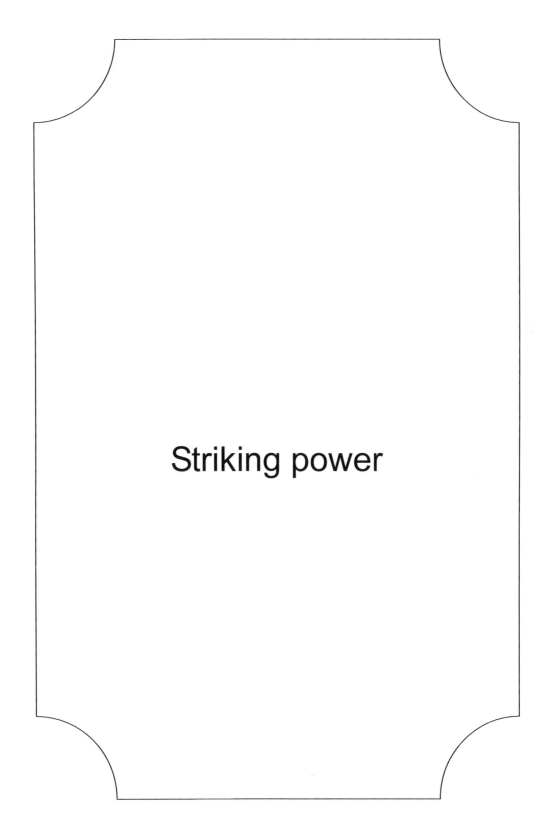

Striking power

US Navy seals 'motto'

"The more you sweat in training, the less you will bleed in battle."

Wall bag striking and punching

A lot of martial artists think that a canvas wall bag is mainly for wing chun, but this is not true, it is a traditional Chinese martial arts training tool that can be used for a full range of strikes and punches from any style of matial arts. They also adorn many wooden dummies, not just wing chun dummies. We have seen them filled and nailed to choy lay fut dummies, praying mantis dummies and even wall dummies in hung gar kung fu schools. They make the perfect striking area or target and provide different densities for a realistic feel.

If you are a beginner then training on canvas wall bags which have been filled with sand or gravel should not be rushed, building strength in the hands, knuckles and wrist takes time and should only be practiced by people over 18 years of age. If rushed in the early stages then it could cause injury and in some cases permanent damage.

Traditional conditioning training many years ago would have to be done at least everyday. Some teachers or masters would even have insisted that you would have to practice condition up to three times a day and at the exact same time everyday. But in the present day, time seems to be at a Permian. To gain a legendary iron palm or iron fist would take a life time of complete dedication just to this cause. But with these set conditioning routines the traditional striking techniques and the combinations that the martial arts experts suggested and that we suggest in this book means that you will be able to maximize your power, learn new striking techniques from a range of traditional Chinese kung fu styles while developing extensive strength behind any strike that you already practice.

Basic striking

We want to take you through these traditional techniques one step at a time. So start by standing in front of the wall bag either side on for jab work or lead punches or square to it for more direct striking, make sure that you are close enough as not to over extend the arm, (when striking, your arm should never be locked to full extend), The punch should hit the target before the arm is fully extended. Knowing that the bag is fixed to a solid wall, you should remember that a great deal of the force from the strike will return back along the arm, so the bag should never be hit with full force, especially by beginners.

Checking the distance, striking with a relaxed arm and practicing putting the power in the last couple of inches, putting all the power in at the last moment is known as 'snap power'. Mastering this technique takes time but when mastered, it will help dramatically increase the effectiveness of your strikes and punches. Another way to train the snap power is to hit the bag hard with full power but from only a couple of inches away.

Different teachers advocate different striking techniques and routines. So we have brought all of these views and ideas together so that you can benefit from their knowledge and expertise.

12 Traditional strikes from Chinese martial arts

Here we have hand picked 12 of the main strikes from different styles of Traditional Chinese martial arts that can be practiced and developed on the wall/conditioning bag.

1. Vertical and horizontal fist,

This is the basic punch behind any martial arts system. A good fist has very little, if any air or gaps between the fingers when fully clenched and the top of the knuckles lines up with the top of the wrist, ensuring that when force is delivered to the knuckles the wrist is in line and does not bend, avoiding injury while delivering maximum power.

A good exercise to square the fist up is to perform push-ups on the knuckles with clenched fists, but not advisable for under 18's

When standing in front of the wall bag whether side on for lead or jab work or square on in a relaxed stance. Start by placing your fist on the bag or area which you are going to strike. Second, visualize the target, third get a feel for the surface and density of the bag and fourth get the distance right. Make sure not to over extend the arm, draw back the arm and drill the punch. Build up the power slowly and remember to develop the snap power and alternate the hands. If it's the top bag (head height) then think where a bouts are you striking, the chin, cheek the nose. Just hitting the bag is all well and good but when you practice your forms or kata then the movements mean something, they are performed for a reason so when you are punching the wall bag, remember visualization.

2. Basic punch number two, horizontal fist, although it is practiced a lot in dojo's and training halls while standing in lines or when practicing form or fighting applications we vary rarely use it in actual combat. Sometimes we might use it as a lead jab but more often than not it will be an almost vertical fist that we end up striking with. This is a good punch to practice as it is ideal for training the top of the knuckle to stay in line with the top of the wrist. When practicing this punch it is easy to over extend the arm (fully locked out) so practice slowly with the right technique and power only in the last two inches. This punch does have a tendency to make the elbow come up level with the fist making your ribs an open target, try keeping the elbow below the wrist otherwise it will lack power.

Vertical fist   Horizontal fist

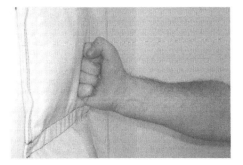 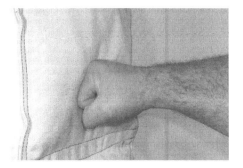

3. Gwi Choy, (back fist).

 To help develop the power for the down ward strike of the back fist, then wall bag training is essential. The back fist is aimed at either the bridge of the nose, chin or cheek bone. It is practiced in a lot of traditional kung fu forms, but sometimes when forms are passed down from instructor to student, this very important striking technique is often lost. Pivoting the arm over the elbow from the chest at first seems to be a strange a move. But if you watch any of the Bruce Lee films, then you will see this primary strike from the kung fu arsenal in action. The turning back fist which is often used in fighting arts such as Thai boxing, kick boxing or MMA fighting is a knock out strike when delivered at the right moment. The light shaded area on the back of the fist (see photo below), top of the knuckles, needs to be conditioned, so drilling strikes on the wall bag either vertically down (see photo below) or horizontal (side ways) is needed....

Back fist striking area   Application

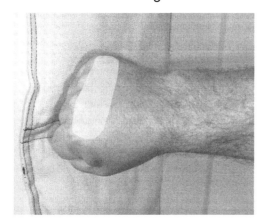 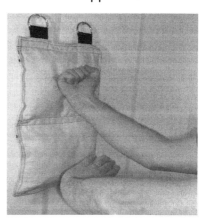

4. Palm strike

When we say palm strike we are really talking about the bottom of the palm. The base of the thumb and across the hand. With all of these strikes it is important to remind you not to over extend your arm when training on the wall bag. The palm strike mainly delivers the power from the shoulder along the elbow and through the base of the palm.

Push-ups with flat palm on the floor are ideal for straightening the hand and developing the right angle with the wrist for an effective palm strike. So when you deliver it for real, it should shoot like a bolt at the target and not a slap. It's primary target is the head and nose or it can have a devastating effect when delivered to the chin at approximately 30 degrees, pushing the jaw onto the garroted nerve will cause instant black out. The elbow can start to rise when this strike is either rushed or you are trying to put to much power into the strike. So master the technique first, take your time and build up the power gradually.

Palm striking area   Application

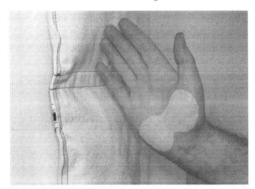 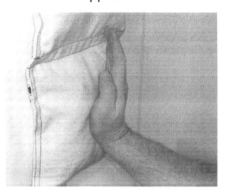

5. Phoenix eye strike.

Striking with the extended knuckle rather than the classic fist can be a devastating punch; it can destroy ribs, damage faces and delivers maximum power when striking pressure points. One of the fingers is moved forwards so that the impact is made with the knuckle, concentrating force onto a smaller area. Some modern martial arts, such as Krav Maga, deliver this strike to the back of the hand while being held. It puts pressure on the small bones in the opponents' hand, causing them to loosen up their fingers in the grip. The wall bag is made for practicing this strike. Hardening the single knuckle and developing the strong fist to support the knuckle does take time, and Because of the penetrating ability of this strike make sure that the wall bag is well filled.

There is nothing worse that hitting the bag penetrating the sand and feeling the solid wall at the back.

Phoenix eye strike   Application

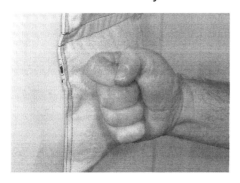 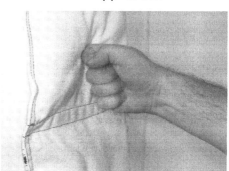

6. Knife hand (karate chop).

 The edge of the hand is a very effective weapon. Primary target areas are the head, across the eyes, nose, throat and various parts of the abdomen. It is often used in breaking demonstration. The knife hand can be used either vertical or horizontal. If striking to the throat or across the eyes then obviously horizontal is best. The wall bags again are made from this type of training. To practice the technique right, it is best to start with the edge of your hand a couple of inches away from the wall bag, relaxing the arm and then generating the power from the elbow, along the arm and then through the wrist, a bit like a whip action, striking the bag with the same snap power as the back fist. Start slowly, get the technique right and then gradually increase power.

Horizontal knife hand   Vertical knife hand

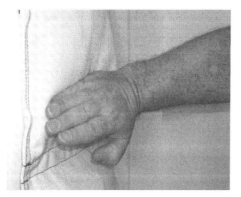 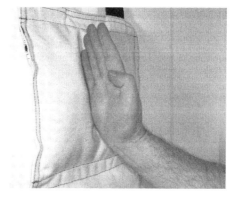

7. Panther fist.

The extended knuckles of the panther fist are a very effective weapon. When delivered properly, It can give a large impact on a small area. Target areas are mainly the ribs, sternum, throat, nose and face. Practice should be done gradually so that the fingers slowly get used to being tightly tucked into the palm. Push-ups on the extended knuckles are a very good way of conditioning the striking area and strengthening the wrist but really only advanced students should practice this, if not practiced properly extended knuckles can easily be broken.

Panther fist   Application

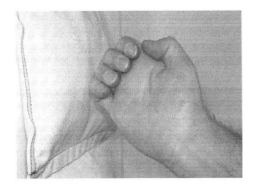 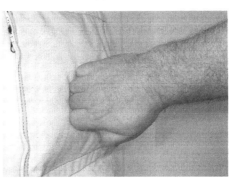

11. Ridge hand strike,

Tucking the thumb into the palm to form a striking surface called the ridge-hand, or reverse knife-hand, As you can see from the photo, the striking area is along the inside of the hand below the first knuckle of the first finger. Ridge-hand strikes are commonly delivered with a hooking motion, or with a straight arm swing. The ridge hand strike is normally used as a last resort, suitable targets include the mastoid muscles of the neck, the jugular, throat, nose, jaw, and the groin. The out come from this kind of strike is not pritty.

Ridge hand striking area   Application

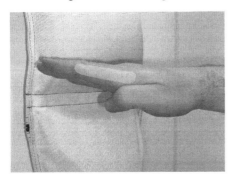 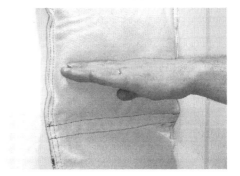

8. Elbow strikes.

An elbow strike in the right area, chin, temple, neck or ribs can drop an opponent straight away. The power generated from the elbow is a lot more powerful that any hand strike, the less joints, elbow, wrist, knuckles that the strike has to travel through then the greater power delivered to your opponent. With this strike there are a few points that need to be clarified. Firstly start training with push-ups. This builds the shoulders, elbow joints and wrist strength. Second when practicing the elbow strike, get the technique right before developing power, do not pivot from the waist when striking, always pivot from the shoulder. If you try to increase power and swing or pivot from the waist, the shock or impact will travel back along the shoulder and into the neck and spine. Always pivot from the shoulder joint and strike with the arm. At first it might seem to lack power but with the right technique you will not need a lot of power.

Start by standing in front of the wall bag approximately eighteen inches away. Lay your right hand on the bag about chest height so that your elbow sticks out to the side and then bring your right hand into your chest while striking the wall bag with your elbow. The waist does not move or pivot round. Try five to ten reps with each elbow to start of with. This strike is covered in more detail further on in the combination drill section of this book.

Elbow strike   Application

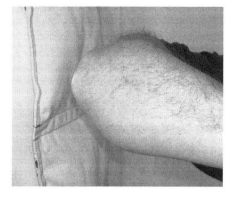 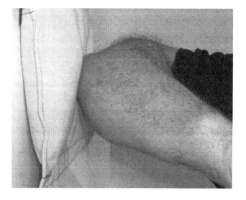

9. Tiger claw.

The striking movements and of the tiger claw style are lightning fast, agile and very powerful. The techniques have a ripping, tearing, clawing and grasping applications.

The face, neck and throat are prime targets for this strike. Start by striking into the sand or gravel bags with the tiger claw hand to condition the finger tips and help develop a strong grip and then throwing a single filled wall or gravel bag to and from your training partner and only catching and tossing the bag using the tiger claw hand is an effective way to condition the hands as well as the fingers and wrists..

Tiger claw

Application

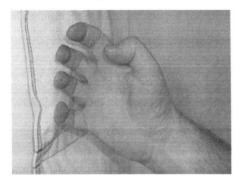
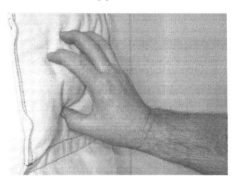

10. Hammer fist.

The hammerfist does exactly what it says. It is sometimes used during "ground-and-pound" striking in mixed martial arts to avoid damaging the bones of the hand. A strike with the bottom of a clenched fist, using an action like swinging a hammer, can also be used horizontally like a backfist strike. This strike is effective against areas on the body and head, hence it is particularly effective for striking the temples, nose, eyes, the wrist (for blocking punches), and striking the sternum and the ears.

Striking area of the hammer fist

Application

11. Finger strike

This strike is sometimes known as the 'spear hand'. It is best practiced on a free hanging small or single section wall bag, enabling the bag to swing when hit so that you do not get the sudden impact and shock running down and injuring the hands knuckles or fingers. Gentle striking against a free hanging sand bag is a good method for target practice as the finger strike or finger jab is mainly aimed at the soft parts of the human body such as the eyes or throat. In our interviews some instructors said that the fingers would be used but close together yet other instructors stated that the fingers would be spread apart so that if the assailant moved, which they generally do then at least one of the fingers would hit the target. we would tend to agree with them as fingers close together are only going to hit one point yet spread apart, they will hit several points.

Horizontal finger strike or (Spear hand)   Vertical finger strike

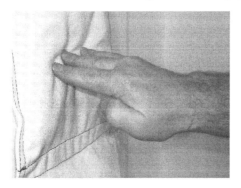 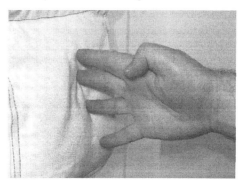

12. Back hand strike or mantis hand

This is also known as a 'feeler strike' or 'mantis strike'. There are only a few kung fu or karate styles that use this striking method. The power in this strike is generated from the wrist as the hand bends down just before impact. The application is often used after a block down with the same hand. It can be used vertically as a upper cut to the chin and nose or dropping the shoulder for the horizontal application striking the ribs and sternum area. The characteristics of the preying mantis fist might look strange but preying mantis kung fu has a long history and the mantis hand strike is very effective and can deliver a powerful strike in a very short distance.

The back of the hands and wrists should be slowly conditioned through gently striking the wall bags with the back of the hand in the mantis shape. Also push-ups on the back of the hand are an effective way to toughen the wrists but only for the more advanced students over 18 years of age.

Striking areas of the paw strike   Application

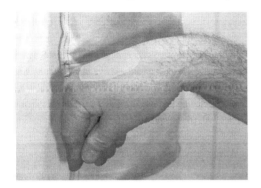 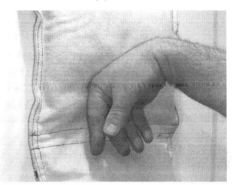

Note

When practicing these strikes or punches there are a few points that all of the instructors and coaches pointed out to us and that you should keep in mind when training. 'Remember to breath and relax' when drilling these techniques. Beginers tend to think that strength and power are the main reason for wall bag training but as we all agree that it is technique first. Tension tends to reduces speed and power as muscles act in pairs in opposition to each other (e.g. biceps and triceps). If the arm is tensed then maximum speed and power cannot be achieved as the biceps will be opposing the extension of the arm. Also unnecessary muscle tension wastes energy and causes fatigue.

Many skilled practitioners pride themselves on being able to generate "short power" or large amount of power in a short space (' snap power') and this can only be achieved with a relaxed mind and body.

Combination drills

Joe Lewis

Everyone has a plan until they've been hit.

Combinations

Hand techniques such as punching, striking or grappling is only one level of martial arts training and practicing it in class is a good start but it is a mile away from actually using these hand techniques in a self defence situatition. When used in real life, on the street when you need to defend yourself. The situation is never quite what you pictured it to be. It is not always how or when you wanted it to happen. Out of all the martial artists that we interviewed and that had actually used their martial arts training in a street or defence situation, ninty five percent said it was over in seconds. There was no fancy moves or jumping spinning kicks like you see in the films. There was no rules or trophys, just bang, bang, bang, over. That quick. In these extreme fight or flight situations there is no time to think, 'what technique shall I use', there is no instructor standing there telling you to do it again until you get it right, there is just reaction.

How do we react

Our reaction and response in life situations are govened by a mixture of fear, past conditioned thought patterns and personal experiences.

When a martial arts instructor teaches a technique to a student. The student practices the technique and hopefully the instructor will watch them practice the technique until they get it right. Until it becomes part of them, part of their martial arts ability. Until it becomes a natural reaction. Sometimes we learn so many technique, so many moves that we will probably never use ninty percent of them, only when we either go through forms or kata, or compete in martial arts competitions. Learning all of these moves, forms or katas helps us to become a more complete martial artist. They help and increase or understanding of martial arts and the art of fighting. All the reserch and interviews that we carried out proved to us that all the traditional training, not just training empty hand but weapons training as well, define a martial artist from a street fighter.

Developing combinations

To help develop these strikes and punches and use them with a free flowing movement. We want to show you the next stage. It covers a series of combinations that will show you how to mix and flow between the different strikes. The importance of working though striking and punching combinations is so that they become second nature, they become a natural reaction, with out thought. To quote a martial arts legened...

'Bruce Lee' ...movement with out thought..

Combination drills

The first of these combination shows two punches with the same hand.

1) Starting with a left cross block with panther strike to the ribs under the opponents arm.

2) Pulling down their arm with a cross block and delivering a back fist to the face or bridge of the nose.

The second combination on page 43, shows three strikes.

1) knife hand to the throat, remember the power is in the wrist.

2) followed by the left cross punch to the head.

3) finished off with the cover block using the left hand and digging into the ribs with a panther strike.

 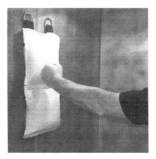 

These first two combinations are easy to follow and quick to learn. They use four of the strikes that we have been practicing in the conditioning and striking chapters of this book. They are direct strikes, not elaborate or fancy moves. You do not even have to adjust your foot work to deliver them.

The main points that the instructors and coaches wanted to point out to students of the fighting arts was one of *Bruce Lee's* core principles' 'simplify movements', keep them direct and simple.

Here is a simple double panther strike with the same hand.

1) Low panther strike to the ribs with a right cross block covering the head,

2) Quickley pulled back while keeping the block in place,

3) Then delivering a panther strike jab to the face.

 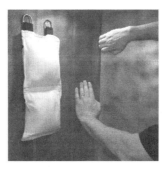 

Here is another good example of double strikes this time aimed directly towards the head.

1) Right cross, straight punch to the chin, note the position of the block covering the body and ready to cover the head.

2) The ridge hand is delivered with a hook motion to the fore head from the left hand side.

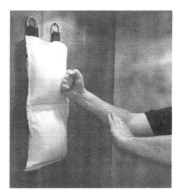 

Here is a combination using two different strikes towards the centerline of the body.

1) Panther fist to the sturnam keeping the block high to cover the head when striking below the lower body.

2) Followed up with a back hand strike to the nose or chin.

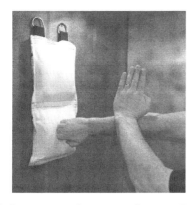 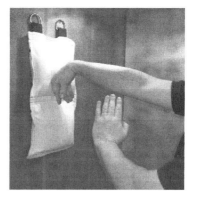

One of the most deverstating strikes in close quarter fighting has to be the elbow strike, its main targets are the temple, face, neck, chin, and the side of the head.

Trying to throw an elbow strike at your opponent from a long distance away is vary hard as the entire body has to move with the strike to give it any power or to connect with its target.

So telegraphing this move is iInevitable with out any distraction. But when performed up close, then this is when the elbow is most effective. So power has to be generated over a short distance.

To generate power behind an elbow strike try this exercise.

1) Lay your hands on the wall bag with slightley bent elbows, so that you only have the set distance to work with.

2) Then slightley moveing towards the bags while twisting your shoulder and striking with your elbow.

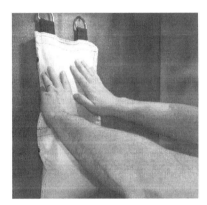 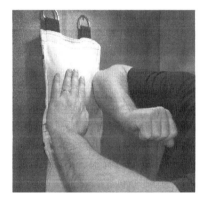

Try working through combination with the same hand and arm. This example shows a right hand punch followed up with a right arm elbow strike

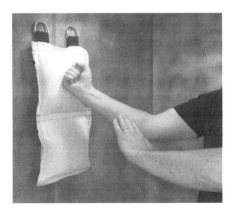 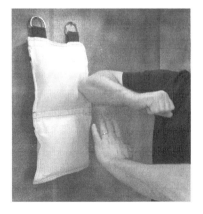

Here is a good example of a technique that would be usful in a street situation. Place your hands on the wall bags as you might do to an aggressive person, as if you are laying them on their chest to keep them at distance then when the time comes collapse the block while striking the chin with the elbow strike. This technique does not take long to learn and after a short period of time even a beginner can generate enough power behind this strike to make it an effective defence technique. It can be practiced against focus pads, punch bags or strike shields but to get a real feel for the impact of the elbow strike, then a sand filled wall bag is what is required.

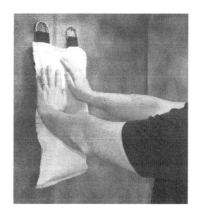 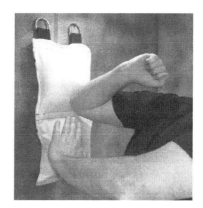

Developing power over a short distance makes the Phoenix eye and panther fist strike to the ribs much more effective.

1) right cross straight punch

2) followed by a short sharpe panther fist or phoenix eye jab to the ribs.

 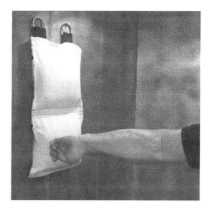

A good example of a rolling combination, is the upper cut. Start with the right upper cut and left hand block then both hands follow over towards you in a circular motion, then the left hand strikes the wall bag with a upper cut and the right hand blocks.

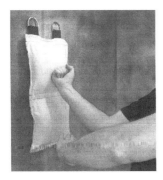  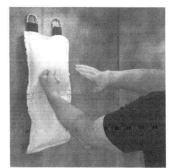

This final example uses a back fist to the face then twists down for a same hand hammer fist strike to the groin area. Short combination like this can be easerly trained and quickly become a natrual reaction for the student.

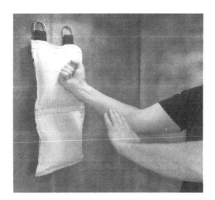 

The whole point of running through these examples of simple combination is to show you how the strikes and punches that you have learned from this book can be easily used and put together. So building up your confidence and to stimulating your imagination. After a short period of time you can become fluid with mixing together any of these traditional striking combinations that you want to practice on the wall bags or need to use.

When you practice the spear hand and as a lot of people have a longer middle finger, it is advisable to slightly bend your middle finger so that it lines up with the other twofingers on either side. This will give you a more powerful spear hand and make this a lot more effective.

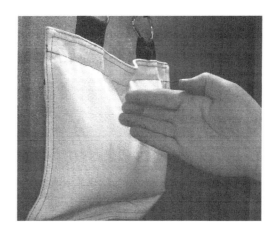

Chain punching drills

Chairman Mao

"Civilize the mind but make savage the body."

Chain punching

Those students that have never practiced chain punching before. The term 'Chain punching' means one after the other. As one strike lands the other hand is cocked ready to punch and then as the hand on the bag leave the target the otherhand starts and so no...Light chain punching drills on the wall bag is a good way of getting a feel for actual contact strikes, developing power, conditioning your hands and perfecting your techniques.

Start slow and pay more attension in the early stages to the hands and the techniques then focus on developing the tension and snap power in the last two inches before impact. Then alternate the section of the wall bag, if you are training on a three section wall bag, work up and down the sections, striking each section twice then three times for each section. If you have different fillings then be aware of the different densities as you move from one section to the other.

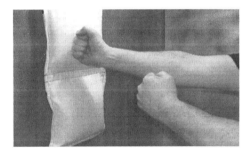 

When chain punching, don't just stick to a straight punch, practice all of the different strikes with a chain punch method.

When chain punching with the panther fist or knife hand. Practice horizontal and vertical strikes as this will quickly build up strength in the wrist.

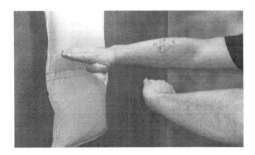 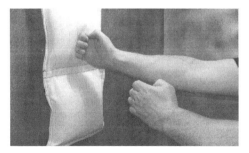

After you have a feel for these different strikes, alternate between them.

Palm and mantis strikes can be practiced in a chain punch format as well but remember that even with these two more traditional strikes, developing the snap power in the last two inches is a key component to making them work.

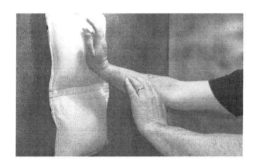 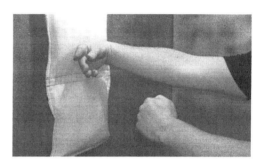

We could carry on and list many more combinations but as we said before*…" This is a book of letters and it is upto you to wright the words "*

What works for you is most important, not if its your instructors best technique or if all of the other students in your martial arts class have mastered a certain technique. It has to suit you, your body type, your ability.

Here is a few important points that we want you to ask your self when training on the wall bags and to consider when working through combinations of your own.

The first is visulisation. Then..

What part of the body am i aiming for (chin, eyes, throat, ribs etc)?

What strike am I using for that area of the body?

How does the punch or strike feel when delivered?

Does it feel natural?

Am I generating enough power?

Am I relaxed?

How is my breathing?

How can I speed up the strike without loosing the technique?

Self improvement is the ability to keep asking yourself questions about you own ability…

We can not strike what we do not see..

We have lost count of how many times we have seen martial artists and instructors either going through a form or demonstrating a technique and their eyes are looking in a completely different direction other than where the punch or strike is heading. They are either looking down towards the ground or up at the ceiling. It might be that they have mastered and taught the technique a thousand times and that they know what or where it is aiming for. But this shows a degree of either arrogance or ignorance and might be a good indicator of the nature of the instructor as well as the senior students. The eyes have to be focused on the target where the strike is aiming. It is a lucky strike that hits a target with out visual awearness of the targets position.

Where shall I focus the power

There are two secrets behind distructive power. The first secret is the obvious one, (1) power generated by either strength or technique.

The second secret (2) is the point of focus. True distructive power is the ability to hit through a target.

When you are throwing a punch, lets say towards the face, your point of focus should not be the face. Your 'distructive power' point of focus should be at the back of the targets head. So to put it bluntly, you punch through the face towards the back of the head.

Ed Parker

"Traditionalists often study what is taught, not what there is to create."

Foot work and body postioning

The instructors and coaches that we interview all had there own views, version and theories regarding footwork and body postioning. From information that we gathered together it appears that the style dictates the theory behind the footwork. Preying mantis pay a lot of attension in placing most of their body weight on the back leg while wing chun keep the stance short with even weight on both legs and yet styles such as hung gar or choy lay fut have a wide open stance. This guide is focused on the traditional sand bag training with perticular emphisis on the dynamics of the traditional hand strikes, there development and application. So what ever your chosen art, wether MMA, Jujitsu, karate, tae kwon do or Kung fu these traditional hand techniques can be conditioned, drilled and perfected to be an added advantage to your fighting art, no matter what style.

Suspended sand bags and target training

"Author unknown"

"That which doesn't kill me, will make me stronger!"

Hanging canvas conditioning bags

Filling a single section wall bag with either sand or gravel and suspending it provideds an excerlent target to practice the more precise techniques such as the mantis or crane strike. It is also easier to condition the finger tips for the spear hand and finger strikes with out the hard impact of striking a wall bag which has been mounted on a solid wall.

A swinging sand bag also makes an ideal tool for target training as well as conditioning.

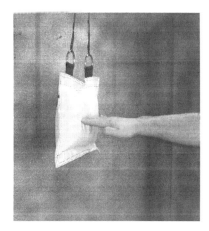

Here is a few examples of traditional strikes from a varity of chinese martial arts styles that the sand filled hanging bag is really suited for. Spear hand above with a finger strike and crane strike below

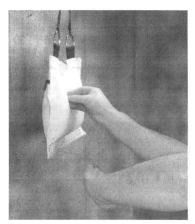

Two other different strikes from traditional styles of chinese martial arts, on the left is the mantis finger strike which mainly targets the eyes and on the right is the tiger claw strike again its main target is the eyes, face and throat.

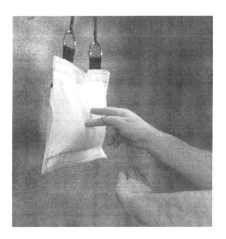 

Through our reserch we came across some interesting training techniques. Especially by the traditional Chinese martial arts schools.

To practice finger strike combinations they suspend a two section wall bag and alternate striking between the two suspended sections.

 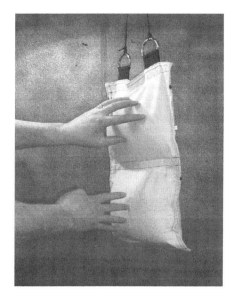

'Chi' Power

Some of the Chinese martial arts instructors that we interviewed said that learning the ability to move the 'Chi' around the body especially when delivering a punch was essential. This ability takes years to master and starts with learning how to deliver the snap power that we mentioned earlier. Most senior martial arts practitioners have some idea about the concept of Chi energy. Chi refers to the natural energy of the Universe, which permeates everything. All matter, from the smallest atoms and molecules to the largest planets and stars are made up of this energy. It is the vital force of life. It is the source of every existing thing. Chi has many manifestations. To the kung fu and taiji practitioners of China it is known as "Chi," but different philosophies and cultures call it by different names. Japanese martial arts call it "Ki." Naturally, in each manifestation the Chi is viewed and defined differently, but basically it is the same thing. It is the power which enables us to think, move, breathe, and live – the power that makes gravity act like gravity. It is what makes electricity electric. It is the link between our perception of the inner and outer worlds. It is our connection to the very flow of the universe and the prime moving force within the human body. Chi is not breath; it is the power that makes it possible for us to breathe. Chi is not simply "energy," it is what gives energy the power to be energy. Chi is the power behind movement and thought…and it is everywhere. It is in the oxygen we breathe and the blood that flows through us.

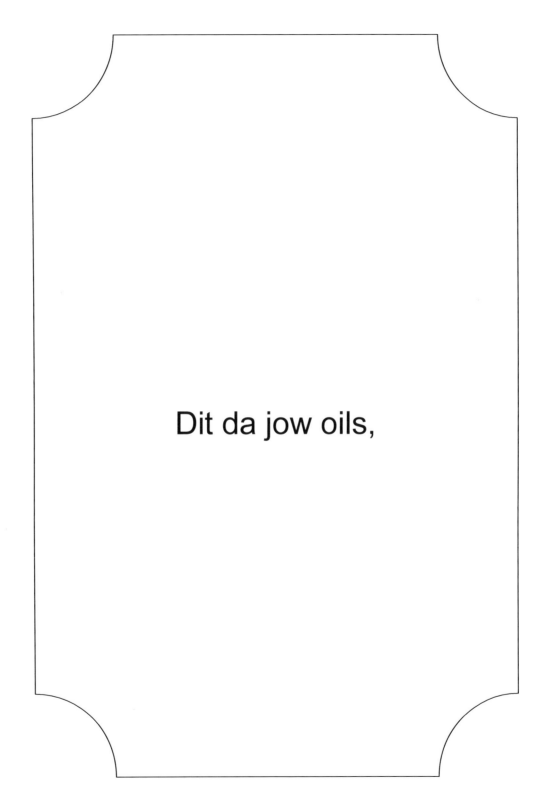

Dit da jow oils,

Buddha

"Your work is to discover your work and then with all your heart to give yourself to it."

Dit Da Jow, oils and balms

Dit da jow, literally translates from Chinese as "steel hit wine". It is an herbal liniment with an alcohol base, used to help the martial artist recover quickly from bruises, **sore muscles and** other minor injuries. It is also recommended for hand conditioning and made from a selection of Chinese herbs. These traditional Chinese remedies for relieving minor aches, tired muscles and swollen tendons also helps condition the skin when massaged into the hands regularly, before and after every hard training session. There are a great number of different recipes for dit da jow, many of which are claimed to be secrets passed down from ancient times. But they are all used in the same basic way. Once it is rubbed in, the alcohol base evaporates away and leaves the herbal ingredients behind. Depending on the recipe sometimes these ingredients can stain the skin. This staining should be left on in order for the herbs to take effect.

The herbal ingredients of the dit da jow may vary and can normally be purchased from traditional Chinese medicine shops in urban areas with large Chinese populations. The names of the herbs used are provided here in Chinese with English translations. They include (but are not limited to): da huang (rhubarb), ru xiang (frankincense), mo yao (myrrh), chuan hong hua (safflower), gui wei, zhi ke, chuan gong, tao ren, mu xiang, chen xiang, jin jie, chi yao, ji geng, zhi zi (gardenia), hu gu, dan pi, hunag bai (phellodendron bark), mo yao (myrrh), dang gui wei (tang kuei tails) and xue jie ("dragon's blood" [a form of red tree sap]).

The most common use of dit da jow is on a bruise or sore spot to relieve the pain and swelling. The practitioner applies dit da jow liberally to the injured area as soon as possible after the injury takes place and rubs it in forcefully. Some martial arts schools encourage the injured person to have a partner rub the dit da jow in, as the partner will do so with greater force, not feeling the pain of the bruise. The extra pressure is used both to ensure the dit da jow is rubbed well into the injured area and as a form of deep-tissue massage this will help prevent swelling before it occurs.

It is important to note that no matter what recipe is used, all dit da jows are for external use only and should never be consumed or used on injuries that involve broken skin. They are also only used for minor injuries and never as a substitute for proper medical care in the case of a major injury. Also, many recipes contain ingredients that may be harmful in large doses, so you should only use dit da jow under the supervision of someone trained in the use of such herbal medicines.

Dit da jow recipe

This is a simple jow recipe that uses common Chinese herbs that are for the most part easy and cheap to purchase.

(These are the botanical names and Chinese names) 1 oz.=30 grams

- 1 bottle of strong vodka, gin or Chinese rice wine
- Artemesia (Liu ji nu) - 5g
- Borneol (Bingpian) - 1g
- Carthamus (Honghua) - 5g
- Catechu (Ercha) - 8g
- Cinnabar (Zhusha) - 5g
- Cirsium (DaJi) - 1g
- Dragon's Blood (Xuejie) - 30g
- Mastic (Ruxiang) - 5g
- Musk (Shexiang) - 1g
- Myrrh (Moyao) - 5g
- Pinellia (ShengBanXia) - 5g

Take all ingredients and grind into a fine powder and add the whole bottle of vodka or gin. If you desire to have the herbs soak, then pour the combination into a dark glass container and place it in a closet or cupboard where it should not get too hot and periodically shake the liniment once or twice a week. You should note that if you do this the traditional way, then the herbs are loosely ground and not ground into a powder.

The longer the Jow sits in the bottle the stronger it will become.

Make sure that you store the jow in a glass bottle and not stored in plastic bottles as over time the plastic starts to break down into the herbal formula.

Please note that this Jow recipe may not be as dark or "smelly" as other jow recipes due to the quality of herbs and time left to soak before usage.

This is a "fast" formula. It's original intent is to be made now to use now, not in a month or two.

It is important that Dit da Jow oils should not be rubbed into open wounds, taken internally or splashed into the eyes.

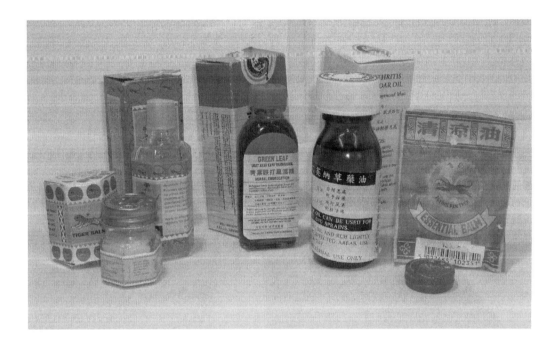

If you can not get hold of the traditional Jow oils then other liniments available which have very good healing properties are Tiger balm, this comes in either red tiger balm (being the hottest) and white tiger balm (menthol properties). Tiger oil (clear rub on liquid). And then there is Thai boxing oil which also has very good healing properties.

Hand Training Equipment

Ursula K. Le Guin

"It is good to have an end to journey toward; but it is the journey that matters, in the end."

Equipment

This book covers conditioning of the hands which are one of the primary weapons of martial arts. So let's take a look at some of the different modern day hand conditioning and strengthening equipment available.

Boading balls are a very good way to keep the hands flexible and maintain natural dexterity. Some boading balls have nice chimes and designs on them. This really makes no difference what so ever. Regular use preferably after wall bag training or any hand conditioning exercises make the boading balls essential.

Makawara boards are the Japanese conditioning tool. Mainly used to condition the knuckles, they were originally made from rope and straw,

They help develop striking ability by letting you experience resistance to punches, kicks and other strikes.

A poor punch will bounce off the makiwara if the body is not in a position to support the energy generated by the strike. It also develops targeting, and focus and the ability to penetrate the target to varying degrees of force. Okinawan methods recommend a regimen of hitting the makiwara 50-100 times per day, with each hand,

Modern day makawara boards are spring loading or thick padding with wood backing. They do have limited use and only have a single density which diminishes as they slowly wear down.

Eagle claw gripper is a spring loaded frame with individual springs and hooks for each finger, this is good for strengthening and working on each finger.

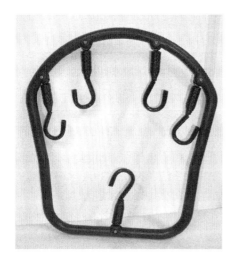 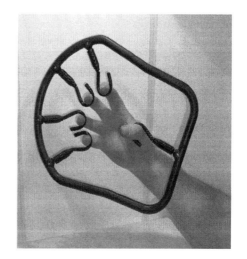

Hand grips are now supplied with different resistances, with metal, wood or plastic handles.

Iron grip trainers were originally designed by Bruce Lee; they are the only grip trainer that uses weights and not spring mechanisms to build and strengthen your grip.

For Chinese martial arts equipment **www.Gwangung.com**

1301040R0

Printed in Great Britain by
Amazon.co.uk, Ltd.,
Marston Gate.